Thoughts from the Garden Gate

A Special Gift

To

Mum

From

Kim

Date

March 1999

Ribbons of Love

A Celebration of Sisters

Christmas Wishes from the Heart

Gardens of Friendship

Happy Is the House That Shelters a Friend

In the Presence of Angels

Just for You: A Celebration of Joy and Friendship

Loving Thoughts for Tender Hearts

Mother: Another Word for Love

Thoughts from the Garden Gate

Thoughts
from the
Garden
Gate

Brownlow
BROWNLOW PUBLISHING COMPANY, INC.

Don't lose Gladness! every hour
Blooms for you some happy flower.
Though be foiled your dearest plan,
Don't lose faith in God and man.

ANONYMOUS

Open the door, let in the air,

The winds are sweet and the flowers are fair:

Joy is abroad in the world today.

BRITISH WEEKLY

They are never alone who are accompanied
with noble thoughts.

PHILIP SIDNEY

I've always been proud of my age.
I think people should be proud they've been around
long enough to have learned something.

FRANCES MOORE LAPPE

The Gardener's Instinct

So deeply is the gardener's instinct implanted
in my soul, I really love the tools with which I work—
the iron fork, the spade, the hoe, the rake, the trowel,
and the watering-pot are pleasant objects in my eyes.

CELIA THAXTER

The butterfly counts not months
but moments and has time enough.

RABINDRANATH TAGORE

As we cry to God, He hears,
and dares us to look at things
from His perspective.

KAREN BOSCH

Fountains of Refreshment

Talk not of wasted affection,

affection never was wasted;

If it enrich not the heart of another,

its waters, returning

Back to their springs, like the rain,

shall fill them full of refreshment;

That which the fountain sends forth

returns again to the fountain.

HENRY WADSWORTH LONGFELLOW

Those who love deeply never grow old;
they may die of old age, but they die young.

SIR ARTHUR WING PINERO

If we are ever in doubt about what to do, it is a good rule to ask ourselves what we shall wish on the morrow that we had done.

JOHN LUBBOCK

The gardens of my youth were fragrant gardens and it is their sweetness rather than their patterns or their furnishings that I now most clearly recall.

LOUISE BEEBE WILDER

If sorrow makes us shed tears, faith in the promises of God makes us dry them.

AUGUSTINE

Happiness is only in loving.

LEO TOLSTOY

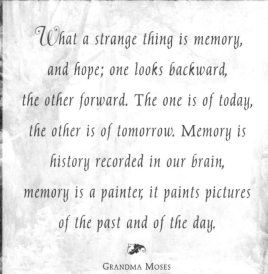

What a strange thing is memory,
and hope; one looks backward,
the other forward. The one is of today,
the other is of tomorrow. Memory is
history recorded in our brain,
memory is a painter, it paints pictures
of the past and of the day.

GRANDMA MOSES

The man who has planted a garden feels that
he has done something for the good of the whole world.

CHARLES DUDLEY WARNER

The joy of the heart colors the face.

ANONYMOUS

Carts Overflowing

You care for the land and water it; you enrich it
abundantly. The streams of God are filled with water to
provide the people with grain, for so you have ordained it.
You drench its furrows and level its ridges; you soften it
with showers and bless its crops. You crown the year with
your bounty, and your carts overflow with abundance.

PSALM 65:9-11

When grace is joined with wrinkles,
it is adorable. There is an
unspeakable dawn in a happy old age.

VICTOR HUGO

One of the worst mistakes
you can make as a gardener
is to think you're in charge.

JANET GILLESPIE

Our Deepest Needs

Our spiritual needs are our deepest needs.

There is no peace till they are satisfied and contented.

The attempt to stifle them is in vain. If their cry be

drowned by the noise of the world, they do not

cease to exist. They must be answered.

L. T. HECKER

A Garden Joy

Is there a joy except gardening that asks so much,

and gives so much? I know of no other except,

perhaps, the writing of a poem. They are much alike,

even in the amount of waste that has to be accepted

for the sake of the rare, chancy joy when all goes well.

MAY SARTON

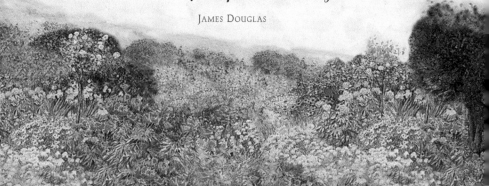

It is good to be alone in a garden at dawn
or dark so that all its shy presences
may haunt you and possess you in
a reverie of suspended thought.

JAMES DOUGLAS

An inexhaustible good nature is one
of the most precious gifts of heaven,
spreading itself like oil over the troubled
sea of thought, and keeping the mind smooth
and equable in the roughest weather.

WASHINGTON IRVING

The things that count most in life
are the things that cannot be counted.

Let nothing disturb you,

let nothing frighten you:

everything passes away except God;

God alone is sufficient.

ST. TERESA OF AVILA

You don't have to light all the world,

but you do have to light your part.

I will be the gladdest thing

under the sun,

I will touch a hundred flowers

and not pick one.

EDNA ST. VINCENT MILLAY

Looking Forward

In all the recipes for happiness I have ever seen,
"something to look forward to" has been given
as an important ingredient. Something to look
forward to! How rich the gardener, any gardener,
is in this particular integrant! For always he
looks forward to something if it is only the
appearance of the red noses of the Peonies in
the spring or the sharp aromas that fill the air in
autumn after the frost has touched the herbage.

LOUISE BEEBE WILDER

To be with those we love is enough.

Ah, how true it is! and it is a happiness

which will outlast this life.

In this thought I love to rest.

MADAME SWETCHINE

Seed Time

Thine is the seed time: God alone

Beholds the end of what is sown;

Beyond our vision weak and dim

The harvest time is hid with him.

JOHN GREENLEAF WHITTIER

Those who have suffered much are like those
who know many languages; they have learned
to understand and to be understood by all.

MADAME SWETCHINE

The love of gardening is a seed
that once sown never dies.

GERTRUDE JEKYLL

A clay pot sitting in the sun will always be a clay pot.

It has to go through the white heat of the furnace

to become porcelain.

MILDRED WITTE STOUVEN

We don't need to be told a great deal.

We just need to be reminded a lot.

MARK TWAIN

I have learned from experience that the greater part
of our happiness or misery depends on our dispositions
and not on our circumstances.

❧

MARTHA WASHINGTON

To stand by the beds at sunrise and see
the flowers awake is a heavenly delight.

❧

CELIA THAXTER

Childlike Hearts

Thy home is with the humble, Lord!

The simple are thy blest;

Thy lodging is in childlike hearts;

Thou makest there thy rest.

FREDERICK W. FABER

Life is the first gift, love is the second,
and understanding the third.

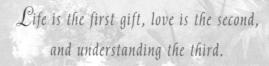

MARGE PIERCY

Watching something grow is good for morale.
It helps you believe in life.

MYRON S. KAUFMANN

Of Dearest Worth

These are the things I prize

And hold of dearest worth:

Light of the sapphire skies,

Peace of the silent hills,

Shelter of the forests, comfort of the grass,

Music of birds, murmurs of little rills,

Shadows of clouds that swiftly pass,

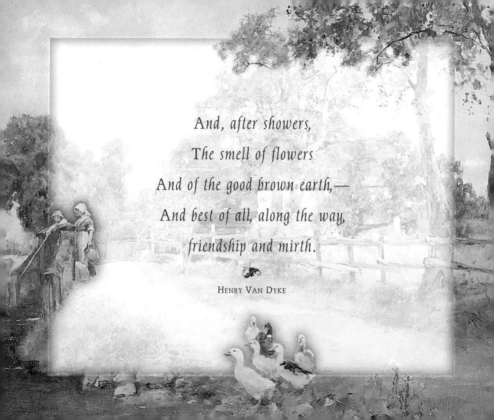

And, after showers,

The smell of flowers

And of the good brown earth,—

And best of all, along the way,

friendship and mirth.

HENRY VAN DYKE

Let your mind be quiet,

realizing the beauty of the world...

The boundless treasures that it holds in store.

EDWARD CARPENTER

Come and see what God has done,

how awesome his works in our behalf!

PSALM 66:5

The commands of God are all designed to make us more happy than we can possibly be without them.

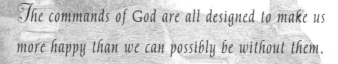

THOMAS WILSON

Buried seeds may grow but buried talents never.

ROGER BABSON

The price and the glory of a mortal's life
is that "we never arrive; we are always on the way."

D. ELTON TRUEBLOOD

The good you do is not lost, though you forget it.

ANONYMOUS

Now he who supplies seed to the sower and bread
for food will also supply and increase your store of seed
and will enlarge the harvest of your righteousness.

2 CORINTHIANS 9:10

Many eyes go through the meadow,
but few see the flowers.

RALPH WALDO EMERSON

For everything you have missed,
You have gained something else.

Ralph Waldo Emerson

Mental sunshine makes the mind grow,

and perpetual happiness makes human nature

a flower garden in bloom.

CHRISTIAN D. LARSON

*If you once loved a garden
that love will stay with you.*

LOUISE DRISCOLL

A Day Well Spent

If you sit down at set of sun

And count the acts that you have done,

And, counting, find one self-denying deed, one word

That eased the heart of him who heard—

One glance most kind,

That fell like sunshine where it went—

Then you may count that day well spent.

GEORGE ELIOT

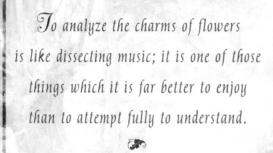

To analyze the charms of flowers
is like dissecting music; it is one of those
things which it is far better to enjoy
than to attempt fully to understand.

TUCKERMAN

There is a miracle in every
new beginning.

HERMAN HESSE

A single thought in the morning may fill our whole day with joy and sunshine or gloom and depression.

PARAMANANDA

All nature smiles, and the whole world is pleased.

DAY KELLOGG LEE

Everything That's Lovely

Bits of sunlight sifting

Down among the trees,

Tranquil stars at evening

Perfume of the breeze,

Roses in the garden

Fresh with morning dew,

Everything that's lovely

Makes me think of you.

B. Y. WILLIAMS

A Tender Plant

Friendship is usually treated as a tough
and everlasting thing which will survive all manner
of bad treatment. But it may die in an hour
of a single unwise word. It is a plant and not
a roadside thistle. We must not expect our friend
to be above humanity.

OUIDA

The thoughts that come often unsought,
and, as it were, drop into the mind,
are commonly the most valuable
of any we have.

JOHN LOCKE

$\mathcal{L}$ove is a tender plant; when properly nourished, it becomes sturdy and enduring, but neglected it will soon wither and die.

HUGH B. BROWN

$\mathcal{M}$ay I never miss a rainbow or a sunset because I am looking down.

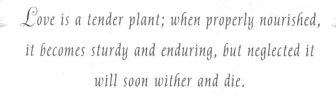

Keep your face to the sunshine
and you cannot see the shadow.

HELEN KELLER

May You Have Enough...

Happiness to keep you sweet;

Trials to keep you strong;

Sorrow to keep you human;

Hope to keep you happy;

Failure to keep you humble;

Success to keep you eager;

Friends to give you comfort;

Wealth to meet your needs;

Enthusiasm to look forward;

Faith to banish depression; and

Determination to make each day better than yesterday.

To Laugh Again

Please, Lord, teach us to laugh again;
but God, don't ever let us forget that we cried.

BILL WILSON

Everything that slows us down
and forces patience, everything that sets us back
into the slow cycles of nature, is a help.
Gardening is an instrument of grace.

MAY SARTON

Grace is the love that gives,
that loves the unlovely and the unlovable.

OSWALD C. HOFFMAN

The righteous...will still bear fruit in old age,
they will stay fresh and green.

PSALM 92:12, 14

He who plants a garden plants happiness.

CHINESE PROVERB

The Way

Who seeks for heaven alone to save his soul,

May keep the path, but will not reach the goal;

While he who walks in love may wander far,

But God will bring him where the Blessed are.

<small>HENRY VAN DYKE</small>

A simple life is its own reward.

<small>GEORGE SANTAYANA</small>

In the long run, we shape our lives,
and we shape ourselves. The process never ends
until we die. And the choices we make
are ultimately our own responsibility.

ELEANOR ROOSEVELT

The greatest gift of a garden is the restoration
of the five senses.

HANNA RION

There is a garden in every childhood, an enchanted place where colors are brighter, the air softer, and the morning more fragrant than ever again.

ELIZABETH LAWRENCE

The glow of one warm thought is to me worth more than money.

THOMAS JEFFERSON

*What makes humility so desirable is the marvelous thing
it does to us; it creates in us a capacity for the closest
possible intimacy with God.*

MONICA BALDWIN

*Gardening is a habit of which I hope never to be cured,
one shared with an array of fascinating people
who helped me grow and bloom among my flowers.*

MARTHA SMITH

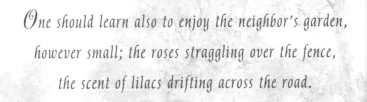

*One should learn also to enjoy the neighbor's garden,
however small; the roses straggling over the fence,
the scent of lilacs drifting across the road.*

❧

HENRY VAN DYKE

Spring unlocks the flowers to paint the laughing soil.

❧

REGINALD HEVER

If you haven't forgiven yourself something,
how can you forgive others?

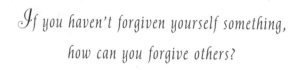

DOLORES HUERTA

Gardening is an exercise in optimism. Sometimes,
it is the triumph of hope over experience.

MARINA SCHINZ

A Few Friends

Give me a few friends who will love me for what
I am, or am not, and keep ever burning before my
wondering steps the kindly light of hope. And
though age and infirmity overtake me, and I come

not in sight of the castle of my dreams,
teach me still to be thankful for life and time's old
memories that are good and sweet. And may the
evening twilight find me gentle still.

AUTHOR UNKNOWN

Love & Friends

Convey thy love to thy friends, as an arrow
to the mark, to stick there; not as a ball against
the wall to rebound back to thee. That friendship
will not continue to the end that is begun for an end.

❧

FRANCIS QUARLES

Only a mediocre person is always at his best.

❧

W. SOMERSET MAUGHAM

No occupation is so delightful to me as the culture of the earth and no culture comparable to that of the garden.

THOMAS JEFFERSON

*They will come and shout for joy,
they will rejoice in the bounty of the Lord—
They will be like a well-watered garden,
and they will sorrow no more.*

JEREMIAH 31:12

Love is like a beautiful flower which I may not touch, but whose fragrance makes the garden a place of delight just the same.

<small>HELEN KELLER</small>

The meaning of life is found in openness to being and "being present" in full awareness.

<small>THOMAS MERTON</small>

Dear Lord, Forgive

If I have wounded any soul today,

If I have caused one foot to go astray,

If I have walked in my own willful way,

Dear Lord, forgive!

To be blind in the eye is better

than to be blind in the heart.

ARABIAN PROVERB

All my hurts
My garden spade can heal.

RALPH WALDO EMERSON

It is always good to know, if only in passing,
a charming human being; it refreshes our lives
like flowers and woods and clear brooks.

GEORGE ELIOT

The late summer garden has a tranquility
found no other time of year.

ANONYMOUS

Threads of Gold

Little self-denials, little honesties, little passing words of sympathy, little nameless acts of kindness, little silent victories over favorite temptations—these are the silent threads of gold which, when woven together, gleam out so brightly in the pattern of life that God approves.

FREDERIC WILLIAM FARRAR

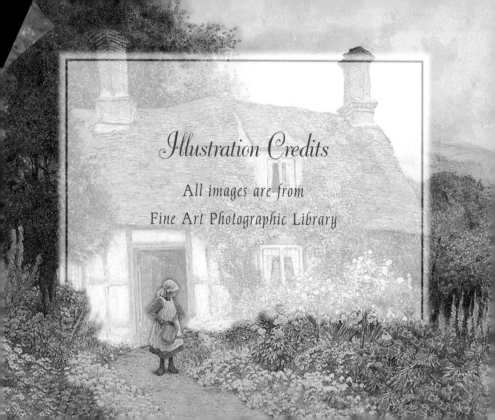

Illustration Credits

All images are from

Fine Art Photographic Library